PREPARATION FOR MARRIAGE

A booklet for those
about to be married

By

R. M. L. WAUGH, M.A., D.D.

London

THE EPWORTH PRESS

Price One Shilling

This booklet has been written in answer to a request for something suitable to pass on to young people about to be married.

The book deals, firstly, with the Marriage Service, the sacredness and value of which are helpfully explained. Then there is a section on the art of living together. Questions such as differences of temperament, health, living with relatives, sex, the only child, the family income, friendships with others, mixed marriages and the secret of a happy home are dealt with in a practical and understanding manner. Finally, a list of books is suggested for further reading. The author has submitted the manuscript to a medical doctor, a psychologist, a minister and a social worker. Much useful guidance is given in a book that never lets the spiritual foundation of married life be forgotten.

PREPARATION FOR MARRIAGE

A booklet for those about to be married

By
R. M. L. WAUGH,
M.A., D.D.

LONDON : THE EPWORTH PRESS

THE EPWORTH PRESS
(FRANK H. CUMBERS)
25-35 City Road, London, E.C.1

NEW YORK   TORONTO
MELBOURNE   CAPE TOWN

FOUNDRY PRESS LTD BEDFORD

CONTENTS

PART ONE

The Marriage Service

PART TWO

The Art of Living Together

The author acknowledges with gratitude valuable suggestions made by a medical doctor, a psychologist, a clergyman, a social welfare worker, and, last but not least, his wife. He is also indebted to writers who have been pioneers in this subject.

PART I

THE MARRIAGE SERVICE

FILMS and novels about love often end with the bride and groom being happily married. But lasting happiness needs spiritual preparation. Therefore you will be well advised to get married in church. Marriage in a Registry Office is purely a business contract and is liable to be broken at any time; marriage in a church is a religious act and implies faith in God to make it a life-long union. There is nothing more tragic than a broken home; and when two young people, with different temperaments and perhaps with unstable characters, decide to get married without seeking God's blessing, their married life is commenced in an atmosphere which cannot ensure their highest happiness. A well-known magistrate with a long experience once said that a happy marriage does not happen by chance: on the contrary, it is the result of forethought, discipline, and effort.

Read carefully what is implied in the Marriage Service and you will see the real significance of coming to church and honouring God, who has put into your hearts a love for each other.

THE CEREMONY ITSELF

The service is very beautiful. Either you may come in together and take your place in front of the Communion rail, or (as is more usual) the bride will come down the left aisle on the right arm of her father or friend. In this case, the bridegroom previously has entered with the best man and waits for the bride. When she has arrived the bridegroom will stand beside her, with the best man on his right side and the bridesmaid and father of the bride on the left. The Law requires the presence of 'two or more witnesses'. After the singing of a hymn (which may be omitted) and a brief prayer, the minister reads the Introduction.

'*We are gathered here,*' he says, '*in the sight of God.*' Here is the keynote of the whole service, which is a religious transaction. If you can realize the presence of God, it will make the service more impressive, and, incidentally, it will relieve you of any nervousness.

THE PURPOSE OF MARRIAGE

Marriage is 'an honourable estate, instituted of God, signifying unto us the mystical union that is between Christ and His Church'. Our Lord quoted with approval the Old Testament words: 'Male and female created He them . . . Therefore shall a man leave his father and his mother, and shall cleave unto his wife: and they shall be one flesh.' As the 'mystical union' between Christ and His Church is very intimate, so it is intended in married life that the personalities of the husband and wife should be deeply inter-blended.

'MUTUAL HELP AND COMFORT'

In the Introduction it is also stated that marriage '*was ordained for the mutual society, help and comfort, that the one ought to have of the other, both in prosperity and adversity*'. Your marriage must not mean the end of your courtship. You should set out to be lovers to the end. There must be the same desire to please each other, the same thoughtful and kindly courtesies and the same eagerness to bear each other's burdens. We shall discuss later the more important adjustments which are needed in a new home.

PARENTHOOD

Marriage was '*also ordained that children might be brought up in the knowledge and love of God and to the praise of His Holy Name*'. If your love for each other is complete, the union may be honoured by the coming of children. As 'Enoch walked with God *after* he begat Methuselah', so you will live near to Christ. Little ones, especially in their earliest years, will catch your sense of values. What a contribution you can make through your children to the welfare of humanity if they are brought up in a Christian home!

ANY LAWFUL IMPEDIMENT

After the Introduction, the minister, speaking to each of you, will ask if there is any reason why you may not be lawfully joined together. You are required by civil law and according to the Church's authority to affirm that you '*know not of any lawful impediment*' why you may not become husband and wife. It is illegal, of course, for a man to get married if he is already secretly married to another woman. Certain other classes also may not marry; for example, those of unsound mind, those under the marriageable age and those included in the table of what is called 'Prohibited Degrees of Kindred and Affinity'. According to the latter, there are thirty relationships (some half-blood and some whole blood) which are forbidden. For example, it is unlawful for a man to marry his son's wife, or his aunt. It cannot be God's will that children should be born of parents whose mental or physical health have been seriously impaired. Any 'unlawful impediment' must be confessed, according to civil law.

7

The minister next proceeds to ask each of you the all-important question : '*Wilt thou have this woman (man) to they wedded wife (husband) to live together according to the law of God in the holy estate of matrimony*ᴰ *Wilt thou love her (him), comfort her (him), honour and keep her (him); and forsaking all other, keep thee only unto her (him) so long as ye both shall live?*' In answering '*I will*', each of you is solemnly promising to be unalterably loyal to each other. You will find after your marriage that physical attractiveness in itself is not an adequate bond of union. Your reliance on God and your deep Christian love will help you to face victoriously the manifold problems of your home life. A sense of humour, too, will enable you to surmount petty annoyances. You will studiously avoid obvious sources of irritation and you will deliberately abstain from finding fault with each other, especially in the presence of your friends and children. Everything must be done to strengthen the ties which bind you to each other.

SACRED VOWS

In the service the man with his right hand takes the woman by her right hand and repeats after the minister the promise : '*To have and to hold from this day forward, for better for worse, for richer for poorer, in sickness and in health, to love and to cherish, till death us do part, according to God's holy law; and thereto I give thee my troth.*' So also the woman, with her right hand taking the man by his right hand, repeats after the minister a similar vow.

You will be here pledging yourselves to let God make your marriage a benediction. The promises are mutual and are equally binding on both the man and woman.

Each partner can be to the other like a lovely tree, giving

8

rest and shelter from the heat and burden of life's troubles.
Wordsworth speaks of the Happy Warrior

> Who, if he be called upon to face
> Some awful moment to which Heaven has joined
> Great issues, good or bad for humankind,
> Is happy as a Lover.
> Which neither shape of anger can dismay,
> Nor thought of tender happiness betray.

The holy and abiding relationship implied in the above
vows is essential if the home is to be an image of the
Kingdom of Heaven and if parents are to be ministers of
God to their children.

THE SYMBOLISM OF THE RING

In the next part of the wedding service we have the giving
and receiving of a ring. After the bridegroom has put it
on the fourth finger of the bride's left hand, he holds it
there and repeats after the minister : *'With this ring, a
token and pledge of the vow and covenant now made
betwixt me and thee, I thee wed in the Name of the Father
and of the Son and of the Holy Ghost.'*

The ring is an outward sign of an inward pledge. It
symbolizes a holy union of body, soul and spirit. As your
marriage is being solemnized in the Name of the Holy
Trinity you will anchor your lives in Him who is ' perfect
love '. True love is ' very patient, very kind. Love knows
no jealousy, love makes no parade, gives itself no airs, is
never rude, never selfish, never irritated, never resentful ;
love is never glad when others go wrong, love is gladdened
by goodness, always slow to expose, always eager to believe
the best, always hopeful, always patient ' (1 Corinthians
13[4-8]).[1] There are some people who like to think that the

[1] Messrs. Hodder and Stoughton, Ltd. have kindly given permission
to use the above quotation from the Moffatt Translation of the Bible,
which is their copyright.

placing of the ring on the minister's book, before it is given to the bride, suggests that it is to be dedicated. Only divine love can make marriage to be crowned with unceasing fidelity.

> ' Love is not love
> Which alters when it alteration finds,
> Or bends with the remover to remove:
> O no! it is an ever-fixed mark
> That looks on tempests and is never shaken;
> It is the star to every wandering bark . . .
> Love alters not with his brief hour and weeks,
> But bears it out even to the edge of doom.'

THOSE WHOM GOD HATH JOINED TOGETHER

After the giving and receiving of the ring, the minister will join together your right hands and ' pronounce ' in the presence of the congregation that you be *man and wife together, in the Name of the Father and of the Son and of the Holy Ghost. Those whom God hath joined together let no man put asunder.* That will be a significant moment. Each of you has doubtless sought God's guidance about the choice of your partner; now you claim His blessing.

THE CONCLUSION OF THE SERVICE

After the actual marriage, the service is continued with a hymn and a passage of Scripture. Not the least important part of the worship is the prayer which the minister then offers that you ' may faithfully live together and may surely perform and keep the vow and covenant betwixt you made, and may ever remain in perfect love and peace togther and live according to God's laws '. There are many things in which you will not see eye to eye; but bear and forbear, never carry the disputes of one day over to the next and always seek to be as attractive to one another as in the days of your courtship.

When the Benediction has been pronounced, you will follow the minister to the vestry, where the Marriage Registry books are signed. For several reasons it is advisable for you to procure a certified copy of the entry of your marriage.

There are some young people who like to have the Communion service after the marriage ceremony. They feel helped in remembering the love which Christ has for them and the power which a sense of His Presence gives. A bride and bridegroom can do nothing more beneficial for their future happiness than at the Lord's Table to ' offer and present themselves, their souls and bodies, as a reasonable, holy and living sacrifice' to their Redeemer and Friend.

THE WEDDING RECEPTION

Some relative or the officiating minister usually proposes the health of the bride and groom. The latter, in his reply, expresses the gratitude of his wife and himself; and then he proposes the toast of the bridesmaids. The best man returns thanks on their behalf. The health of the parents of the bride and groom is sometimes drunk. By having soft drinks and not alcoholic liquor served at the reception, other young people who are present will not be led into temptation and a Christian witness will be borne.

PART II

THE ART OF LIVING TOGETHER

THE PROBLEMS OF MARRIED LIFE

SOMEONE has said that married life is like a jig-saw puzzle. Each piece has its own shape, but all the parts are meant to form one complete whole. So, the husband and wife, the son and daughter, who have found the secret of living happily together, constitute the ideal Christian home.

Domestic happiness can be found through Christian insight and through the patience and love that come from experience. A husband and wife must fully know each other. Generally speaking, there is a difference in the personality of a man and a woman. A man's mind is occupied with public interests and he arrives at his conclusions by reasoning; whilst a woman's mind is generally absorbed in smaller though important matters, and she reaches her conclusions by intuition. It is interesting, for instance, to observe at a Parliamentary General Election how much keener men are than women to listen-in to the latest results. Temperaments also differ. Usually a woman is more easily moved to laughter or tears.

Though all this may be true as a general rule, the opposite is often a fact. The woman may be endowed with public gifts and be alive to world issues. The man may be more sensitive than his wife. It is, therefore, all the more important that you should know each other's outlook and temperament. Not only, then, can possible sources of irritation be avoided, but also such things can be said and done as will strengthen the ties of domestic happiness.

In some countries each of the engaged is entitled to receive a certificate of health about the other from a medical authority. Apart from hereditary tendencies and disabilities, it is highly important that young people contemplating marriage should be medically overhauled. How often ill-health has cast a shadow over a home! The question of health, of course, has a vital bearing on the rearing of children.

The kindliest of 'in-laws' can prove a menace to the happiness of a home. Where it is impossible for a bride and groom to have a house of their own, they should be allowed to live together in a separate part of the house. No matter how well-intentioned a mother-in-law may be, she should avoid giving advice or interfering with the running of a new home. In later years the presence of elderly relatives may have a helpful influence, and the memory of their early love will thereby be kept fragrant.

Psychologists have discovered from numerous interviews that unhappy marriages are most often caused by ignorance or by imperfect understanding of the delicate physical relationships of wedded life. You will find Dr. Helena Wright's book *The Sex Factor in Marriage* helpful here. Indeed, it is because of ignorance and because so many young people are allowed to grow up feeling that there is something revolting and shameful about sex, that it is recognized on all sides today that the facts of life should be taught to the young child in as natural and as beautiful a manner as possible.

It is presumed that you have had a free and frank talk together regarding sex questions. It has happened that a man and a woman have been very fond of each other; but when they have got married the very idea of physical relationship was unbearable to one or other of them: In such a case, frank discussion separately or together with a trusted doctor may help to straighten things out.

The cause of this may simply be some mal-adjustment or ignorance of the right technique. The fault may be with the husband rather than with the wife. It is wise to seek the advice of a medical authority; for in certain cases the cause of the apparent sterility can be removed.

If this is still not successful, the adoption of a child may be considered. This course is a wise one even with those who could have a family but who fear that the health of the mother would be endangered or that some physical or mental disease would be inherited.

For those who suffer this privation, freedom from home ties will allow more time for outside activities, and there are many opportunities for work amongst young people in church and other organizations. Those who are denied parenthood will thus be able to mother and father other people's children.

LIMITATION OF THE FAMILY

Unless there is some sound reason for it, those couples who refuse to have children are laying up for themselves a bitter disappointment for the days to come. It is God's will that every healthy married man and woman should share His creative power. There is danger even in the indefinite postponement of parenthood. A well-known neurologist is of the opinion that such an attitude tends ultimately to weaken that mutual physical attraction which first leads young people to become intimate friends. Moreover, it should be remembered that the presence of little ones in the home calls forth the tenderest human sympathies in the parents; and when the family is grown up, the later years of the father and mother will be enriched by the visits of grandchildren and the care of loving relatives.

Sometimes parents say that they cannot afford to have more than one child. In having just the one, they consider that they can give him the best education and the brightest prospects in life. But how easy it is to overlook the fact that the nursery is a more important sphere of education than the university. An only child is in danger of growing up to be unsociable, introspective and lonely. If he is the victim of a possessive parent there is the great likelihood that in later life he will be unable to make decisions for himself, and to take risks without first consulting his father or mother. It has been said that the over-mothered child offers a moral and psychological problem hardly less acute than the neglected one. To give him a first-class education is very important; but to have the noblest qualities of his character developed and strengthened is even more necessary.

Sometimes the economic reason is stressed by parents whose real motive in limiting their family is a disguised form of selfishness. Those people who are out for ' a good time ' will discover that it is not by refusing to have children that such an experience is achieved, but rather by rearing a family which in later years will be the light and life of the home.

If your first child is born one or two years after your marriage, your personalities will be enriched. If the interval between each child is not less than two years, the mother will have a fair opportunity of recovering her normal health. To leave a gap of four or more years may cause the older child to be jealous, because he has grown accustomed to a privileged position. Favouritism is both foolish and injurious. In later years it may create psychological problems.

Every parent should learn the art of correcting a child's mistakes. Grave harm is sometimes done by hasty and unjust punishment. Any friction between parents can have a most injurious effect on the child. On the other hand, the spiritual mood of the parents can soon be caught even by an infant. If a fretful nurse can depress a baby, a prayerful mother can inspire him. The religious atmosphere of a home has a lasting effect.

BIRTH CONTROL

Many married people use birth-control devices (see book—"Parenthood, Design or Accident" referred to on back cover). Such husbands and wives, to avoid the strain of abstinence and to space out their children, use contraceptives to consummate their deep love for one another.

On the other hand, to practice birth control from motives of selfishness, luxury and sensuality is strongly to be condemned. Parenthood is one of the purposes of marriage; and it should not be evaded, unless on medical advice. A husband and wife should think out their attitude prayerfully and in the light of Christian principles.

THE FAMILY INCOME

Whatever income you intend to marry on, you should decide beforehand how it should be spent. Though the money may be earned by the husband, it should be considered as belonging also to the wife. It is a wise thing to decide how much money should be apportioned to housekeeping and clothes, how much to the Church and charity, and how much to luxuries and holidays. If a husband has a good income, he should put aside something every week for 'the rainy day'. Obtaining furniture and other home necessities through the hire-purchase system often imposes such a burden as is not removed till the furniture is nearly worn out.

Careful consideration should be given to the matter of expenditure, lest the cloud of debt should darken the home. Nothing ruins a home more insidiously than gambling; and football pools often lead people to take the first step on that perilous course. ' The love of money is a root of all kinds of evil.' (1 Timothy 6^{10}.)

TO HAVE A LIFE-LONG FRIEND——BE ONE

Seeing that a husband's duties necessitate his absence from home for most of the day, it is all the more important that everything should be done to strengthen the ties of friendship during the hours that he is at home. If his wife lives in a new district, she is bound to miss her old friends as well as the privileges of her previous business; and, therefore, life can be very lonely during the day. When the husband returns in the evening, he will remember that his wife has been toiling in his absence. It has been said there is no trade union for mothers; their work is never done. The husband will therefore give as much help as he can, especially in carrying coal into the house, lighting fires and washing up. On the other hand, the wife will bear in mind that her husband has to attend to his business at stated times, and punctuality in the serving of meals will be appreciated. Though he will interfere as little as possible with the domestic duties of the home, he will expect that his wife will have a competent knowledge of food values and be more than a ' tin-opener '. If a young woman lacks the necessary knowledge, she would be well advised to join some cookery class or take a course of lectures in domestic science.

In every new adventure there is a temporary thrill. It may be the first flight in an aeroplane or the first experience of a motoring holiday. It is similarly so with two people who begin to explore each other's personality. Mr. C. S. Lewis has described this 'being-in-love' as 'a sort of explosion that starts the engine going. The real thing is something far deeper—something you can live on'.[1] The love that endures must not only be rooted in the emotions, but also in the mind and in the will. Everything must be done to deepen the feeling of 'togetherness'. Even though a husband wishes to take up some hobby or game, to which he had been previously devoted, he should still seek for opportunities of sharing his leisure hours with his wife. It may be a walk together or an evening at a concert. Few women like bowls or football, but they can at least take enough interest in them to be able to converse about them. Few men, on the other hand, care to go near a millinery shop, but what pleasure is given when a new hat is appreciated!

It is easy to get into a rut. A husband becomes absorbed in his newspaper and the wife makes an idol of her house. One hurries out to his club and the other sits alone with her sewing. There is no club to be compared with one's own fireside. How immeasurably richer married life would be if there were cultivated a common interest in literature or sport, gardening or poultry-keeping, civics or politics! Many a happy hour can be spent over a catalogue of urgently-needed seeds for the garden or favourite records for the gramophone; or, a television programme is shared. We have heard of a husband and wife who made it a regular practice to attend certain university lectures,

[1] In his book, *Christian Behaviour* (Geoffrey Bles, The Centenary Press). By whose kind permission this quotation is used.

which they subsequently discussed. When there were no such lectures, they read books by their fireside. The glow of their early comradeship was delightfully preserved all through their lives. Attachment to a local Church with its meetings and social activities can also be both profitable and enjoyable.

FRIENDSHIPS WITH OTHER MEN AND WOMEN

There is no reason why old friendships should not be kept in repair after marriage. The charm of married life will be enhanced and made more secure by fellowship with early acquaintances. Of course, it will be acknowledged at the outset, that a husband and a wife will always have first place in each other's affection. It is sometimes a distressing fact that, owing to the influence of a possessive mother, a young husband or wife will seek refuge in the old home when some misunderstanding arises. If two partners have undertaken solemn vows to live together, they must stand by each other and adjust their differences in a friendly manner. Each must implicitly trust the other in such matters as letters from and contacts with friends. Secrets must not be divulged and suspicions must not be entertained. It is easy for two young people to live a selfish life. Jealousy and self-pity poison many a home. Let self-pity be directed to others. As well as welcoming your friends, entertain lonely people and strangers.

If for any reason (such as the slovenly appearance of the wife or the want of attention on the part of the husband) a friendship develops with someone of the opposite sex outside the home, this course may be arrested by remembering three things : [1] (i) What was the original and sacred marriage vow? (ii) Have not many

---

[1] The author is indebted for this suggestion to W. E. Sargent in his book, *The Psychology of Married Life* (Independent Press).

19

good qualities been overlooked in the other partner? (iii) If children are born will not this infidelity injure their moral and physical health? Such adjustments ought to be made so that an unbroken family may later be filled with happy memories of shared burdens and grateful children.

The Lambeth Conference and the British Methodist Conference have issued a warning against marriages between Protestants and Roman Catholics. One of the grounds of a successful marriage is spiritual unity between the partners. This cannot be achieved in the marriage of Protestants and Roman Catholics without sacrifice on the one side or other of vital principle or some part of their religious faith and practice. Protestants believe that the religious foundation on which a home rests should be the free choice of the partners. This is denied by the Roman Church, which encourages the Roman Catholic member to do his or her utmost to win the other partner to the Roman faith. Moreover, the Protestant is compelled by the priest to give a promise in writing that all the children born of the marriage will be brought up as Roman Catholics. What a strain is placed on a Protestant parent when he (or she) is regarded as a heretic in his own home and he is not allowed to teach his own children the Scriptural truth which he himself was taught! Because of the inevitable discord, no Protestant who values his faith and freedom and who seeks a happy home can contemplate a mixed marriage.

But there is another form of a mixed marriage which is also regrettable, and that is when one parent is a professing Christian and the other is a mere nominal one. If you happen to be in the second category, be assured of this, that nothing can help you better to climb the steep hills of life, bear its heavy burdens over difficult ground and press cheerfully on than a full and deliberate committal of your life to Christ as your personal Saviour, Friend and Guide. The art of achieving domestic happiness demands serious thought and noble ideals. The supreme quality of fidelity is not found in a Registry Office. It is significant that in these days when a wave of secularism is passing over the world, there should be such an alarming number of divorces and such a threat to the very institution of marriage.

COMMANDMENTS FOR THE MARRIED

The Methodist Recorder published some time ago ten rules which were drawn up by one of the judges of the American Supreme Court, after he had heard thousands of divorce cases. His ten commandments are:

(1) Avoid the first quarrel.

(2) Don't argue, nag or find fault.

(3) Let there be no boss rule in the house.

(4) 'Ours' and not 'mine' should be the home possessive pronoun.

(5) Confine your intimacies to yourselves: don't share them with your friends.

(6) Don't live with your in-laws. No matter how humble, have a home of your own.

(7) A little love and affection, as you used to display during your courtship days, will prevent many petty quarrels.

(8) Husbands must keep in mind that running the household is a tough, tedious and tiresome job. Be considerate, and don't overlook the wife's 'nerves'.

(9) Keep respect for each other. When respect goes, love vanishes.

(10) Protect the home with love insurance by having as many children as you can afford.

As a husband, remember that your wife likes to be well dressed. Pay her an occasional compliment. Give her a present. As a wife, remember that your husband likes a nice meal and appreciates punctuality. Let each be tactful, sympathetic and cheerful.

Intimate fellowship with Christ and an earnest desire to do His will have enabled many a husband and wife to overcome such insidious enemies of happiness as deception and jealousy, selfishness and irritability. Never let alcoholic liquor—even in the form of so-called medicated wines—enter your home. Drink brings sorrow and poverty in its train. Make your home a haven of love and service.

In all human love there is a root of selfishness. One wants the wireless on, the other wants to read quietly. One wants to sit up late, the other prefers to retire early. One likes to go to the cinema, the other prefers football. One is fond of spending money on things which the other regards as extravagant. If one acts as a dictator, the other is grieved and full of self-pity. Healing can be found for this conflict of wills. Multitudes of husbands and wives have found happiness and harmony in accepting a higher will, which is God's. Let every problem be brought to Him.

> ' Our wills are ours we know not how;
> Our wills are ours to make them Thine.'

Just as when different pieces of coloured glass are made into a stained-glass window, so when our many duties and relationships, our emotions and impulses are drawn together

22

into one whole in Christ, can the effect be joyous and beautiful.

Never let a day pass without lifting your hearts to God in prayer; seek His guidance. Cultivate a system of Bible reading. Join 'the International Bible Reading Association' or 'the Bible Reading Fellowship'. Your minister will order the daily readings for you. Keep in close touch with your Church. Unless illness prevents you, never let a Sunday pass without attending the House of God. Honour the Lord's Day; make it a hallowed and a joyous one for your family. Judge everything according to the mind of Christ.

Do you remember reading in a lovely story (*Adam Bede*) the words of Dinah Morris to her new-found lover: 'Adam, it is the Divine Will. My soul is so knit to yours, that it is but a divided life I live without you.' Then George Eliot makes this suggestive comment: 'What greater thing is there for two human souls than to feel that they are joined for life—to strengthen each other in all labour, to rest on each other in all sorrow, to minister to each other in all pain, to be one with each other in silent, unspeakable memories at the moment of the last parting.'

YOUR MARRIAGE—A PUBLIC OCCASION

As your wedding will take place in the presence of two witnesses and a congregation, it has a social value. Queen Elizabeth the Queen Mother said that if our homes are truly Christian, then their influence will spread like leaven through all the aspects of our social, industrial, and political life. It is interesting to recall that Horace, the great Roman poet, admitted that whatever good there was in his life was due to his father. Similarly, J. M. Barrie paid tribute to the gracious influence of his mother, whose Christlike character guided him through life. Will you think seriously of the quality of living that will radiate from your home?

'HOME, SWEET HOME'

In a certain house a husband and wife often quarrelled and did not speak to one another for weeks. Then the former found Christ. His children soon noticed how his bad temper and irritability disappeared. Later his wife felt challenged. Her little girl asked her why she could not become like her Daddy. The mother, who often marched in peace processions and sought for unity in the world, confessed that by insisting on having her own way she was causing friction at home. When she accepted Christ and sought to obey Him every day, the home emerged from gloom into sunlight and from chaos into order. Now, every member is sending out a kindly influence into a troubled world. The same priceless gift of Christ and His love can also be yours!

May God crown your lives with His joy; and may your pathway in life be as 'the shining light that shineth more and more unto the perfect day'!

BOOKS FOR FURTHER READING

About to Marry. Douglas W. Thompson. (Epworth Press.) 3/6.

Successful Marriage. A. Herbert Gray. (Rich and Cowan.) A book on the art of achieving happiness in marriage, 5/-.

Guide to Marriage. Leslie Tizard. (Geo. Allen and Unwin.) 8/6.

The Sex Factor in Marriage. Helena Wright. (Williams and Norgate.)
A valuable book on sex technique, 4/-.

Parenthood—Design or Accident. Michael Fielding. (Williams and Norgate.)
A practical handbook on birth control, 4/-.

Men, Women and God. A. Herbert Gray. (S.C.M.)
A very useful guide to right conduct in sexual matters, 5/-.

Abundant Living. E. Stanley Jones. (Hodder and Stoughton.) Spiritual guidance in overcoming life's difficulties, 8/6.

Bible-Reading Fellowship. 171, Victoria Street, Westminster, S.W.1: 2/- for daily Bible Readings for a year.

Talks to Boys and Girls on Sex. Alliance of Honour, 112-114, City Road, London. E.C.1., 3d. each.

Further books can be secured from the Department of Social Responsibility of the British Council of Churches, 56, Bloomsbury Street, London, W.C.1.

The National Marriage Guidance Council 78, Duke Street, Grosvenor Square, London, W., can also afford valuable help.

For further Reading

Whom God Hath Joined
   A Book of Christian Marriage.
   By David Mace, M.A., B.Sc., Ph.D.   *cloth* **6s.** *net*
                                         paper covers **2s. 6d.** *net*

About to Marry
   By Douglas W. Thompson   **3s. 6d.** *net*

Christian Courtship
   By C. J. Clarke   *paper covers* **9d.**

From all booksellers

LONDON: THE EPWORTH PRESS